ENGIN GOLD STAR CLASSICS

Beauty and the Beast

Jeanne-Marie Leprince de Beaumont

engin

Retold by
Uğur Gürses

Edited by
Zeynep Yağmur Mert

Designed by
Türkay Göksoy Zenginer

Pictures by
Kemal Yargıcı

ISBN: 978-975-320-574-0

Published in Dumat Ofset
First Published in September 2016

ENGİN YAYINEVİ
Selanik Cad. 28/6 Kızılay 06650 ANKARA
Telefon: (0312) 419 49 20-21
Belgeç: (0312) 419 49 22
e-posta: info@enginyayinevi.com.tr
http://www.enginyayinevi.com.tr

Beauty And The Beast

About The Author

Jeanne-Marie Leprince de Beaumont

She was born in Rouen, 1711. She loses her mother at the age of eleven. Her family is very poor. Several of her siblings are adopted.

She teaches small children. She becomes famous as a singing teacher. She starts to write moral stories and poems for children. These stories are based on fairy tales. She writes her famous *Beauty and the Beast* in London.

The Story

There is an old merchant. He is very rich. He has three sons and daughters. Beauty is the most intelligent and the beautiful daughter. One day, they become very poor. The merchant needs to go and find his ship. He intends to be rich again. However, he finds himself in a palace. A beast lives in this palace. The old man becomes his capture.

The Characters

The Beast	is very ugly.
Beauty	is the best of all her siblings.
Beauty's father	tries to do the best for his children.
The Prince	is handsome.
Queen	is able to hug her son in the end.
The Stately Lady	is a magical character.
Beauty's sisters	are jealous of Beauty.
Beauty's brothers	do not want to let Beauty go back to the Beast.

Introduction

Once upon a time, there is a very rich family. One day, they become very poor. The father of the family hears some good news from the port. He wants to go to the port to get his treasure. Then, he meets the Beast and the adventure begins.

The Rich Merchant

Once upon a time, there is a very **rich merchant**. He has three sons and three **daughters**. The merchant's children are very **lucky**. They can have **whatever** they **wish**. They live happily. They can buy **toys**, they can eat good food, they can **travel** in the country and they can do everything.

The youngest daughter is different from the **others**. She is the most **moderate** one. She is **considerate**. She doesn't wish much. She is very beautiful. For this reason, the other sisters don't like her very much. They are **jealous** of her.

One day, a misfortune **befalls** the family. Their house **catches** fire. It **spreads** fast and all the **furniture**, books, pictures, **gold**, **silver** and **precious goods** burn. This is not the end. In addition to this, the merchant loses every ship upon the sea. **Pirates loot** his ships. Some ships **sink** and some ships are on fire. **Furthermore**, some of his workmen in distant countries **betray** him. At last he loses all his **wealth** and he becomes a very poor man.

The merchant has a little house and the merchant has to **move** there. The kids are very unhappy. They **are not used to** this difficult lifesytle. They move from a big house in the city centre to a very small house in the **countryside**. They have everything before, but they have nothing now. They have many friends before, but they have no friends now.

The boys start to **cultivate** the field. The girls start to do the **chores**. They live like **peasants**. Their clothes are **muddy** and dirty now. They always **complain** about their new life. Only the **youngest** girl tries to be brave and cheerful. She is also sad when she hears about these **misfortunes**. **However**, she manages to **overcome** these difficulties. She always tries to **make jokes** and amuse her father and **siblings**. She tries to persuade her sisters to join in dancing and singing.

"Why are you so **cheerful**? We are very poor but you are still dancing," say the girls to the youngest one.

"**Come on**! **Let's** dance! I know we are poor. But we need to be **strong**," says the youngest girl to the others.

She is much **clever** and **prettier** than the others. She is so lovely and everyone calls her Beauty.

Good News

Two years pass. The merchant and his family **get used to** their new life. One day, the merchant **receives** good news. One of his ships comes **safely** to the **port**. The kids are **excited**. They say, "**Hurray**! Our **poverty** ends. This ship is full of **treasure**. We are rich again." The kids want to **set out** directly for the port and find the ship.

Their father is **prudent**. He doesn't **rush**. He says, "I want to go first. I can find the ship."

Beauty has **doubts** about her father's trip. **Everybody** in the family thinks that they are rich again but Beauty.

The merchant **gets ready** for the trip and sets out. All the kids want something from him. One wants a beautiful dress, the other wants **jewels**. They think they are rich and their father can buy these things after getting the treasure from the ship.

Beauty is watching her **greedy** siblings in the corner. She is **silent**. She doesn't want anything from her father. The merchant sees her and asks, "Don't you want anything, dear?"

“I don’t want anything. I only want you to come back home safely, father,” says Beauty. The merchant feels happy.

“Please! Choose something and I bring it for you,” says the merchant. ”Ok Dad! Please **bring** me a **rose**. There aren’t roses here. I love them so much,” says Beauty.

Meeting With The Beast

The merchant arrives at the port. He finds the ship, however, there is no money or treasure around. The captain of the ship spends all the money during the two-year journey. The merchant is **still** poor.

The merchant **decides** to go back home. The weather is so bad. On his way back home, he becomes **exhausted** with cold. It starts to snow and the merchant finds a **cave**. He stays there during the night. In the morning, he **wakes up**. **Everywhere** is **covered** with thick snow. He is lost now. He doesn't know where to go.

He **accomplishes** to open a **path** in the **thick** snow. He walks for a very long time. He is so tired. Suddenly, he sees a splendid **castle**. This castle seems very strange. Everywhere is covered with snow, but there is no snow around the castle. Instead, there are **flowers** and **fruit trees** everywhere.

He goes to the castle. It is warm and **pleasant** in the castle. He is hungry. He walks and searches everywhere in the castle but he sees nobody to ask for food. He is tired and sleepy. Finally, he stops **roaming** the castle and finds a small room. A clear fire is burning in the room and there is a **couch** near the fire. The merchant falls asleep.

Next morning, the merchant wakes up. The sun is shining. He is still hungry. Suddenly, he sees a **tray** full of breakfast on a small table. Hot, fresh coffee, **sweet bread rolls**, jam, fruit and fresh cream. He is **shocked**. He shouts, "Can anybody hear me?" There is no reply to him. He eats everything on the table.

He sleeps all the night but he is still tired. He falls asleep again. In the afternoon, he wakes up. This time, there is a **delicious** lunch on the table. He is surprised. He is very hungry and he has the lunch. There is still nobody around.

After lunch, he waits for somebody to come. Nobody **appears**. He starts to walk **around** the castle. He sees beautiful roses in the garden. He remembers Beauty's wish and decides to take one for her. **Immediately**, he hears a **strange** noise.

"You are very **ungrateful**. I save your life, I give you food and bed. In return, you steal my roses. I **value** these roses more than anything in the **universe**. I can kill you for this," says the Beast to the merchant.

The merchant looks at the Beast. He is like an animal. He is very ugly. The merchant is scared of him. He falls on his **knees** and says, "Please **forgive** me My Lord! I don't want to **offend** you. This rose is for one of my daughters."

"My name is not My Lord. I have a name. I am the Beast. I don't love **compliments**. I want people to speak as they think. You say you have daughters. I can forgive you if one of your daughter comes here **willingly** and **suffer** for you. You have three months. Either your daughter comes here or I find you to kill." says Beast to the merchant.

The Beast is very ugly. The Merchant doesn't want to give any of his daughters to him. He **accepts** the Beast's offer. He wants to save his life for this time. He wants to see his daughters for the last time.

Coming Back Home

The merchant takes a horse from the Beast's **stable** and he is back home in a few hours. His children are around him. He is not happy. He looks at his kids and **bursts into tears**. At the same time he is holding a rose branch in his hand.

"Here, Beauty! Here is the rose! This rose costs me a **fortune**," says father to the children. He tells them about The Beast and his fatal **adventure**.

Beauty listens to his father and she agrees to go to the castle. She wants to save her father's life. **On the other hand**, her father doesn't want her to go there.

"I am an old man. I have not long to live. The Beast can kill me. But you are all too young!" says the merchant.

Three brothers do not want to lose their father or sisters. They say, "**Nobody** is going to the Beast. We can kill the Beast."

"Never think about this. He is so strong. You can't do anything to him," says the old merchant.

Two sisters **hate** Beauty. She wants to have a rose instead of beautiful dresses or other things. The rose causes another great trouble to the family.

Beauty **insists on** going to the castle. The other daughters are happy about this.

Beauty Goes To The Castle

Beauty and her father are ready to go to the castle. Her father is still trying to **persuade** her not to go there. Beauty is firm. They **mount** together with the horse. They arrive at the castle. There are **fireworks** all around the castle. The sky is **shining** even it is nighttime. It is like a party.

The merchant takes his daughter to the small room. He stays here before. There is a fire here again. The table is set for **supper**. They are very hungry. They start to eat something.

Beauty is happy and making jokes. She wants to **cheer** her father. Suddenly, they hear footsteps. These footsteps clearly belong to the Beast.

Beauty sees the Beast. She trembles at the sight of the Beast. She makes a great effort to hide her horror. She **salutes** him respectfully.

"Good evening, old man! Good evening, Beauty!" says the Beast.

The merchant can't say a word, but Beauty **responds firmly**.

"Good evening, Beast," says Beauty.

"Are you here willingly? Are you going to you be happy to stay here when your father goes away?" asks the Beast.

Beauty answers **bravely**. She is prepared to stay willingly.

"I am pleased to hear that. As you come here willingly, you can stay. As for you, old man, you can leave at **sunrise** tomorrow. When the bell rings, get up quickly and eat your breakfast. Take the same horse. You can never see my palace again. Take your father to the next room," says the Beast. "He can choose gifts for your brothers and sisters," He says goodbye to father and daughter, then leaves.

Beauty is very sad because her father is to leave next morning. She is afraid of the Beast. She obeys the rules. She takes her father to the next room. The room is full of jewels, **splendid** dresses and **ornaments**. They decide to take gold. They think gold is more useful. They put lots of gold into the bags. They are very heavy.

The next morning, the bell rings. It is time for Beauty's father to leave. Two horses are waiting outside. One of the horses is **loaded** with two trunks, and the other is for the merchant to ride. The merchant leaves the castle. Beauty is very sad. She comes to her room and starts to cry. Then, she falls asleep.Beauty has a dream in her sleep. A very handsome prince comes to her and talks to her.

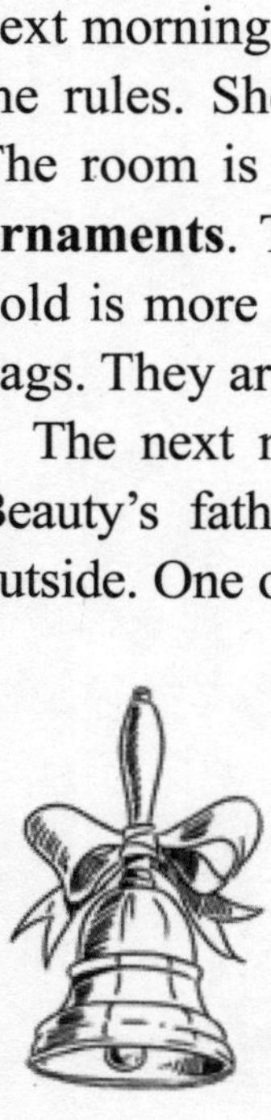

"Ah, Beauty, you are not an **unfortunate** girl. You do something good for your father. Your every wish is going to come true. Try to find me! I love you a lot. Happiness is very close to you." says the prince to Beauty in her dream.

"What can I do to make you happy, Prince?" asks Beauty to the prince.

"Only be **grateful**. Don't trust **appearances**. Don't **desert** me until you save me," says the prince to Beauty.

Beauty wakes up. She finds the dream very interesting. Beauty starts to talk to herself, "I can make him happy. It seems, this horrible Beast keeps the prince a **prisoner**. How can I help him? But after all, it is only a dream. This may not be true. I can do something else to amuse myself."

Will You Marry Me ?

At night, the Beast comes to see Beauty. “Do you enjoy being here, Beauty?” asks the Beast.

Beauty answers cheerfully and she manages to hide her terror. “Yes, I do. I am having fun. Everything is so beautiful,” says Beauty.

“Do you love me, Beauty? Will you marry me?” asks the Beast.

Beauty is afraid. She doesn’t want to make the Beast angry. “Oh! What can I say?” says Beauty.

“Say yes or no without fear,” says the Beast.

“Oh, no, Beast,” says Beauty hastily.

“Ok. Good night Beauty,” says the Beast.

“Good night Beast,” says Beauty. She is happy. This answer doesn’t make him angry. Beast leaves. Beauty goes to bed. She starts to dream of the handsome prince again.

In her dream the Prince talks to her again, “Ah, Beauty! Why are you so unkind to me? I fear my fate is being unhappy forever,” says the prince to Beauty.

Life in the Castle

The castle is a very interesting and **magical** place. Beauty meets magical things everywhere. When she gets hungry, she goes to her room. The meal is ready there on the table. When she wakes up, she finds herself in a very beautiful dress. When she likes something, this comes true suddenly.

One day, she sees beautiful birds in the garden. She likes them a lot. Then she says to herself, "Some of these birds make good friends to me." Then she goes to her room. There are beautiful birds flying and singing in her room.

There is magic everywhere in the castle. There is everything in the castle to make Beauty happy.

Every night, the Beast visits Beauty. He asks the same question to Beauty, "Will you marry me? Beauty answers the Beast with the same answer," "Oh, no, Beast!" Then Beast leaves, Beauty sleeps again. She dreams of her prince. She always hears the same words in her dream, "Do not trust appearances. Trust your heart. Let your heart **guide** you." These words are always in her mind.

Beauty Misses Her Family

One day, the Beast makes his usual visit to Beauty. Beauty seems very sad.

"What is the matter, Beauty? Why are you so sad?" asks Beast to Beauty. Beauty is not afraid of him. He has **ferocious** look and **dreadful** voice. However, he seems **gentle** to Beauty.

"I wish to see my home and my family," says Beauty. The Beast seems sad and starts to cry.

"Ah, Beauty. Please do not leave me! What else can I do to make you happy? Do you hate me? Do you want to **escape** from the castle?" asks the Beast.

"No, dear Beast. I don't hate you. Let me go for two months. I miss my family a lot. I **promise** to come back and live here forever." says Beauty.

"This costs my life but I don't want to make you sad. Take four boxes and fill it whatever you want. Please come back here after two months. If you don't come, I die. Two months later, touch this ring and say that you want to go back to the castle. You can be here at that moment. Good night, Beauty!" says the Beast.

Beauty takes four boxes. She **fills** them with rare and precious things. Then she goes to sleep. In her dream, she sees her beautiful prince again.

The prince seems sad.

"What is the matter?" Beauty asks.

"Why are you leaving me?" asks the Prince.

"Ah, I am only going to visit my father. I want them to see I am safe and happy. I promise to come back. If I don't, the Beast dies," says Beauty to the Prince.

"Why? Is the Beast so **important** to you?" asks the Prince.

"I feel unhappy if I don't care of him. He is ugly but this is not his fault," says Beauty.

Suddenly, she hears a voice. She wakes up. She is in a room. The room seems different from the ones in the castle. She sees the boxes. Then she hears her father. She is at her father's home.

With The Family

Her family is **astonished** to see Beauty back home. They ask a lot of questions to her. She tells them about the Beast and the castle. Beauty's sisters and brothers tell her about their lives in her **absence**.

"I need to go back to the castle two months later." says Beauty. When her brothers and sisters hear this, they **lament** loudly.

She is back home but nothing **amuses** her. She misses the castle.

—❋—

One day, in her dream, she sees the Beast. He is lying on the palace garden. He is about to die. Suddenly, a stately lady appears, "Ah, Beauty! You see what happens when people don't **keep their promises**! If you don't come, the Beast is going to die," says the lady.

When she wakes up, she makes up her mind. She decides to go back to the castle. She says goodbye to everyone and she turns her magical ring. She says she wishes to go back to castle and see the Beast again. Then, she falls asleep.

She wakes up. She sees her beautiful room in the castle. Her birds are singing and they are happy to see her again.

Beauty wants to see the Beast. There is nobody around. She searches all the rooms. She goes to the garden. She can't find him. She calls him loudly. There is no answer. She continues to search. Finally, she finds him. He is **lying** on the ground. The scene is the same as it is in her dream. She touches his head, but the beast doesn't move. He seems dead.

"Oh, he is dead. It is all my **fault**," says Beauty.

She checks his breath. **Fortunately**, he is breathing. She goes and **fetches** some water. She **sprinkles** it over his face. The Beast comes round.

"Oh, Beast, I am frightened! I now understand that I love you!" says Beauty.

"Can you really love me? I am such an ugly creature. You are just in time. You keep your promise. Now go and have some rest. We meet again. Bye for now," says the Beast.

At supper time, the Beast and Beauty meet again. Beauty tells him about her family. She thanks the Beast for letting her go home. After supper, the Beast stands up and before he says goodbye to Beauty, he asks again, "Will you marry me, Beauty?"

"Yes, dear Beast," answers Beauty.

Suddenly, a **blaze** of light springs up before the palace; fireworks **crackle** and guns **bang**. There seems a writing in the sky, "Long live the prince and his bride."

The Beast changes into the handsome prince that Beauty sees in her dream.

At that moment, a **chariot** lands on the **terrace**. There are two ladies. One is the **stately** lady in her dream, the other is the queen.

"Well, Queen, this is Beauty. She rescues your son from the terrible **enchantment**. They love each other. Will you let them marry?" says the stately lady to the queen.

"I consent with all my heart," says the queen. "How can I thank you Beauty? You save my son," says the queen to Beauty.

Beauty's family also join to the wedding. Beauty and the prince live happily ever after.

THE END

GLOSSARY

***(pl.):** Plural noun

absence	yokluk, mevcut olmama
accepts, (to) accept	kabul etmek
accomplishes, (to) accomplish	başarmak
adventure	macera
amuses, (to) amuse	eğlendirmek
appearances (pl.), appearance	dış görünüş(ler)
appears, (to) appear	görünmek, ortaya çıkmak
be used to	alışık olmak
around	etrafında, civarında
astonished	şaşırıp kalmak
bang	silah sesi
befalls, (to) befall	başına gelmek
(to) betray	ihanet etmek
blaze	alev
bravely	cesurca
bread rolls (pl.), bread roll	yuvarlak ekmek(ler)
(to) bring	getirmek
bursts into tears, (to) burst into tears	gözyaşlarına boğulmak

castle	kale
catches, (to) catch	yakalamak
cave	mağara
chariot	at arabası
(to) cheer	neşelendirmek
cheerful	neşeli
chores (pl.), chore	ev iş(ler)i
clever	akıllı, zeki
Come on!	Haydi!
(to) complain	şikâyet etmek
compliments (pl.), compliment	iltifat(lar)
considerate	düşünceli
couch	kanepe
countryside	kırsal bölge
covered	kaplı
(to) crackle	çatırdamak
(to) cultivate	ekip biçmek
daughters (pl.), daughter	kız çocuk(lar)
decides, (to) decide	karar vermek
delicious	lezzetli
delighted	memnun, hoşnut
(to) desert	terk etmek
doubts (pl.), doubt	şüphe etmek
dreadful	ürkütücü
enchantment	büyü
(to) escape	kaçmak
everybody	herkes

everywhere	her yer
excited	heyecanlı
exhausted	yorgun
fault	hata
ferocious	gaddar, acımasız
fetches, (to) fetch	gidip getirmek
fills, (to) fill	doldurmak
fireworks (pl.), firework	havai fişek(ler)
firmly	kararlı bir şekilde
flowers (pl.), flower	çiçek(ler)
(to) forgive	affetmek
fortunately	neyse ki
fortune	servet
fruit trees (pl.), fruit tree	meyve ağacı (ağaçları)
furniture	mobilya
furthermore	dahası
gentle	nazik, kibar
(to) get used to	alışmak
gets ready, (to) get ready	hazırlanmak
gold	altın
goods	mal, eşya
grateful	minnettar
greedy	obur, açgözlü
(to) guide	rehberlik etmek
(to) hate	nefret etmek
however	fakat

hurray	yaşasın
immediately	hemen
important	önemli
insists on, (to) insist on	ısrar etmek
jealous	kıskanç
jewels (pl.), jewel	mücevher(ler)
(to) keep their promise	sözünü tutmak
knees (pl.), knee	diz(ler)
(to) lament	yas tutmak
let's	haydi
loaded	yüklü
(to) loot	yağmalamak
lucky	şanslı
lying, (to) lie	uzanmak
magical	sihirli
(to) make jokes	şaka yapmak
merchant	tüccar
misfortunes (pl.), misfortune	talihsizlik(ler)
moderate	ılımlı
(to) mount	(ata) binmek
(to) move	taşınmak
muddy	çamurlu
nobody	hiç kimse
(to) offend	kırmak, incitmek
on the other hand	diğer yandan
ornaments (pl.), ornament	süs eşyası (eşyaları)

others	diğerleri
(to) overcome	üstesinden gelmek
path	patika
peasants (pl.), peasant	köylü(ler)
(to) persuade	ikna etmek
pirates (pl.), pirate	korsan(lar)
pleasant	memnun, hoşnut
port	liman
poverty	yoksulluk
precious	değerli
prettier	daha güzel
prisoner	mahkûm
(to) promise	söz vermek
prudent	ihtiyatlı
receives, (to) receive	almak
responds, (to) respond	cevap vermek
rich	zengin
roaming	gezinmek
rose	gül
(to) rush	acele etmek
safely	güvenli bir şekilde
salutes, (to) salute	selamlamak
shocked	şaşkına dönmek
(to) set out	yola çıkmak
shining, (to) shine	parlamak
siblings (pl.), sibling	kardeş(ler)
silent	sessiz
silver	gümüş

(to) sink	batmak
splendid	harika
spreads, (to) spread	yaymak
sprinkles, (to) sprinkle	serpmek
stable	ahır
stately	etkileyici görünümlü
still	hâlâ
strange	tuhaf
strong	güçlü
(to) suffer	acı çekmek
sunrise	gün doğumu
supper	akşam yemeği
sweet	tatlı
terrace	teras
thick	kalın
toys (pl.), toy	oyuncak(lar)
(to) travel	seyahat etmek
tray	tepsi
treasure	hazine
unfortunate	talihsiz, şanssız
ungrateful	nankör
universe	evren
(to) value	değer vermek
wakes up, (to) wake up	uyanmak
(to) wish	dilemek
wealth	varlık, zenginlik
whatever	her türlü
willingly	kendi isteğiyle
youngest	en genç

ACTIVITIES

Match The Characters

The Beast	thanks Beauty to save her son's life.
Beauty	brings the queen to the castle.
Beauty's father	are jealous of Beauty.
The Prince	want to kill the beast.
Queen	loses his wealth.
The Stately Lady	wants to have one of merchant's daughter.
Beauty's sisters	falls in love with Beauty.
Beauty's brothers	goes to the castle to save her father's life.

TRUE / FALSE

1. The Beast changes into a prince in the end. T F
2. The merchant wants Beauty to go to the castle. T F
3. Beauty is a moderate girl. She doesn't wish much. T F
4. The Beast has a magical castle. There are magical powers in the castle. T F
5. The stately lady brings the queen to the castle on a chariot. T F

6. Beauty wants golden jewels from her father on his trip to port. T F
7. Beauty's brothers want to kill the Beast. T F
8. The Beast wants to make Beauty happy. T F

Comprehension Questions

1. Does the Beast become happy at the end of the story?
2. Does Beauty want to get married with the Beast in the end?
3. Can Beauty's family join the marriage ceremony?
4. Is the merchant rich again at the end of the story?
5. Who saves the Beast's life?
6. What does the merchant want to take from the Beast's garden?
7. How many siblings does the Beauty have?

Make Sentences

1. is / a / lunch / delicious / there / table / the / on/.
2. changes / the / into / Beast / handsome / a / prince/.
3. dreams / Beauty / of/ handsome / prince / the/.
4. sisters / always / Beauty's / their / about / poverty / complain/.
5- chariot / brings / queenly / a / the / lady/.

Multiple Choice

1. Beauty keeps her .... and comes back to the castle.
   a. treasure   b. promise   c. costumes

2. The merchant wants to get a .... from the Beast's garden.
   a. fish   b. bird   c. rose

3. The queenly lady thanks to ....
   a. the Beast   b. Beauty   c. the merchant

4. The Beast is very ....
   a. rich   b. poor   c. rude

5. The Beast wants to get one of the merchant's ....
   a. brothers   b. daughters   c. sons

6. Everywhere is covered with snow but the ....
   a. merchant's house   b. castle   c. port

7. The Beast is like an animal and he is very ....
   a. handsome   b. ugly   c. poor

8. Beauty sprinkles .... on the Beast's face and he comes round.
   a. milk   b. fruit juice   c.water

9. The merchant loses everything, but one day, one of his .... comes back to the port.
   a. ships   b. brothers   c. cavaliars

10. The castle is a .... place.
   a. bad   b. magical   c. dirty

Answer Key

Match the Characters

The Beast	wants to have one of merchant's daughter.
Beauty	goes to the castle to save her father's life.
Beauty's father	loses his wealth.
The Prince	falls in love with Beauty.
Queen	thanks Beauty to save her son's life.
The Stately Lady	brings the queen to the castle.
Beauty's sisters	are jealous of Beauty.
Beauty's brothers	want to kill the beast.

TRUE / FALSE

1-T	2-F	3-T	4-T
5-T	6-F	7-T	8-T

Comprehension Questions

1. Yes, he becomes happy at the end of the story.
2. Yes, Beauty wants to get married with the Beast in the end.
3. Yes, they can join to the ceremony.
4. Yes, the merchant is rich again at the end of the story.
5. Beauty saves the Beast's life.
6. The merchant wants to get a rose from the garden of the Beast.
7. She has five siblings.

Make Sentences

1. There is a delicious lunch on the table.
2. The Beast changes into a handsome prince.
3. Beauty dreams of the handsome prince.
4. Beauty's sisters always complain about their poverty.
5. A chariot brings the queenly lady.

Multiple Choice

1-b	2-c	3-b	4-a	5-b
6-b	7-b	8-c	9-a	10-b

STAGE 1

Gulliver's Travels

Jonathan Swift

Retold by Suzy Usanmaz

Gulliver's Travels is one of the best known works of Jonathan Swift and a classic of English Literature. The novel is about Gulliver's travels to four different places and his adventures with different people and creatures he meets during these travels.

Pocahontas

Retold by Suzy Usanmaz

Pocahontas is a story of a native American woman who is a daughter of Powhatan, the chief of a native tribe in Virginia. During the discoveries of the New World, a group of English soldiers come to Virginia. The native people want to protect their land against foreigners. The foreigners are powerful with their guns whereas the native people have only arrows and physical strength. However, both sides learn many things from each other. Pocahontas becomes a symbol of peace during this struggle. She falls in love with John Smith; however, John Smith does not want to marry Pocahontas, so she marries another English soldier, John Rolfe and goes to London. Her story becomes a legend.

STAGE 1

Aesop's Fables

Aesop

Retold by Suzy Usanmaz

Aesop's Fables is the collection of fourteen well-known fables of Aesop. The author makes his readers think about morality and other virtues while entertaining them. In this collection you can find the stories of the Tortoise and the Hare, the Ants and the Grasshopper, the Bundle of Sticks and many others.

Tale of Peter Rabbit and Other Stories

Beatrix Potter

Retold by Suzy Usanmaz

This book is the collection of four stories of little bunnies and other animals. Peter Rabbit is a naughty rabbit who gets into trouble. His cousin Benjamin Bunny tries to save his children from the farmer Mr. McGregor and Mrs. Twittlemouse wants help from Mr. Jackson because of the bees.

STAGE 2

Frankenstein

Mary Shelley

Retold by Suzy Usanmaz

This is the story of Doctor Frankenstein who creates a monster by putting different parts of dead bodies together. The monster does not have bad intentions; however, including Dr. Frankenstein, everybody gets afraid of his ugly and frightening appearance and runs away from him. Although the creature wants to help people, he is treated cruelly. Thus, he becomes angry and takes revenge on his creator, Dr. Frankenstein.

Little Women

Louisa May Alcott

Retold by Suzy Usanmaz

This is the story of four sisters, Meg, Jo, Beth and Amy. They are poor, but happy. Their father, Mr. March is a soldier who is fighting in the Civil War. Their mother teaches the girls to help people. This is the story of a family who lives together bonded by love.

STAGE 2

Just So Stories

Rudyard Kipling

Retold by Suzy Usanmaz

In this book you can find interesting stories in which you can learn about how leopard got his spots, why elephants have got long noses, why cats are lazy, how rhinoceros had a new skin and the power of a mongoose.

Heidi

Johanna Spyri

Retold by Suzy Usanmaz

This is the story of an orphan, little girl whose name is Heidi. After her parents' death, Heidi starts to live with his grandfather and has a new friend, Peter. She likes the mountains and is happy to live there. Then she goes to Frankfurt to live with an ill girl who is Clara and they become friends. Clara visits Heidi on the mountains and gets well.

STAGE 1

1 Gulliver's Travels
2 Pocahontas
3 Robin Hood
4 Andersen's Fairy Tales
5 Pollyanna
6 Little Prince
7 Alice in Wonderland
8 Aesop's Fables
9 Wizard of Oz
10 Tale of Peter Rabbit
11 Puss in Boots
12 Grimms' Fairy
13 Peter Pan
14 Winnie the Pooh
15 Hans Brinker, or the Silver Skates
16 Beauty and the Beast
17 Rebecca of Sunnybrook Farm
18 Ethan Frome
19 The Prince and the Pauper
20 Twenty Thousand Leagues Under the Sea

STAGE 2

21 Treasure Island

22 Little Women
23 Around the World in 80 Days
24 Frankenstein
25 Journey to the Centre of the Earth
26 Rip Van Winkle / Sleepy Hollow
27 Heidi
28 Mysterious Island
29 Just So Stories
30 The Secret Garden
31 Anne of Green Gables
32 Five Little Peppers and How They Grew
33 Story of the Treasure Seekers
34 Sherlock Holmes
35 The Odyssey
36 Arabian Nights
37 The Moonstone
38 Christmas Books
39 The War of the Worlds
40 The Time Machine

STAGE 3

41 The Adventures of Huckleberry Finn
42 Tom Sawyer
43 The Call of the Wild

44 Robinson Crusoe
45 Dr. Jekyll and Mr. Hyde
46 The Phantom of the Opera
47 Kidnapped
48 The Hunchback of Notre Dame
49 The Thirty Nine Steps
50 The Metamorphosis

STAGE 4

51 Oliver Twist
52 The Three Musketeers
53 Don Quixote
54 Romeo and Juliet
55 Moby Dick
56 O Henry's Short Stories
57 The Man in the Iron Mask
58 The Turn of the Screw
59 Tom Jones
60 Martin Eden

STAGE 5

61 David Copperfield
62 The Count of Monte Cristo
63 Rose